GW01091472

A-Z of Living for Christ

Compiled by
Rev Nick Donnelly

*All booklets are published thanks to the
generous support of the members of the
Catholic Truth Society*

CATHOLIC TRUTH SOCIETY
PUBLISHERS TO THE HOLY SEE

Contents

Dedicated to Damian and Stephen,
brothers by birth and brothers in faith

Picture credits: All pictures from shutterstock.com p.10 © Savvapanf Photo, p.12 © Suprun Vitaly, p.14 © lozas, p.16 © Mordechai Meiri, p.18 © Thoom, p.20 © Antonio Gravante, p.22 © Vibe Images, p.24 © Renata Sedmakova, p.26 © Bukhta Yurii, p.28 © Taiga, p.30 © Purino, p.32 © beer worawut, p.34 © VanderWolf Images, p.36 © wideonet, p.38 © jorisvo, p.40 © Stocksnapper, p.42 © Bill Perry, p.44 © graja, p.46 © James Saunders, p.48 © Luis Santos, p.50 © Rawpixel.com, p.52 © Renata Sedmakova, p.54 © Pavel Bernshtam, p.56 © Renata Sedmakova.

ISBN 978 1 78469 155 4

The secret to living a good Christian life

Pope Francis knows the secret to living a good Christian life, and he wants to share this secret with you. How can we tell that the Holy Father really knows this secret? Look at his irrepressible desire to talk about Jesus and pray; his youthful enthusiasm; his joy in life, and, his care for the poorest and weakest - these are all signs of it. If we want to live a good Christian life, Pope Francis knows that we must fall in love with God. While he is the first to admit he still makes mistakes and is a sinner, Pope Francis is clearly a man who has fallen in love with God and has stayed in love with him. The Holy Father has been described as having "a big heart open to God and to others."

Pope Francis talked about falling in love with God in one of his homilies to the young people in Poland at World Youth Day 2016. He was talking about what inspired Zacchaeus, the tax collector, to climb the tree in Jericho in order to see Jesus:

> Zacchaeus was a public figure, a man of power. He knew that, in trying to climb that tree, he would have become a laughing stock to all. Yet he mastered his shame, because the attraction of Jesus was more powerful. You know what happens when someone is so attractive that

we fall in love with them: we end up ready to do things we would never have even thought of doing. Something similar took place in the heart of Zacchaeus, when he realised that Jesus was so important that he would do anything for him, since Jesus alone could pull him out of the mire of sin and discontent. The paralysis of shame did not have the upper hand. The Gospel tells us that Zacchaeus "ran ahead", "climbed" the tree, and then, when Jesus called him, he "hurried down". [1]

I remember my own 'Zacchaeus' moment when I realised that Jesus was so important I never wanted to leave him. It was the moment I was overcome by the attraction of God. I was a young teenager growing up in south London. It was Holy Week and I was an altar server during the Easter Triduum liturgies at Holy Cross church, Carshalton. I remember being overwhelmed by the stillness, the solemnity, the emotion of the Good Friday liturgy. The sanctuary at Holy Cross is dominated by a more than life-size Crucifix built into the wall. The white figure of Christ in his agony hung from a jet black cross. Listening to the Gospel narrative of the Passion, taking part in the veneration of the cross, receiving Holy Communion, recessing from the sanctuary in total silence, the presence of Jesus was suddenly so real to me. I didn't want to leave him. When I returned home I went to my room and slowly prayed again the prayers of the liturgy and the Passion narrative so that I could stay with him. I was overwhelmed by his love for me.

Pope Francis encourages us to "make space for God's love so he can change you". Looking back I can see that that my participation in the Good Friday liturgy was the beginning of my falling in love with Jesus, drawn by Our Lord's overwhelming love from the cross. The Holy Father explains how to make space for God's love this way:

The Lord thinks of what he will do and of how he will rejoice with his people. It's almost as if he has a dream. He has a dream. His dream is about us. "Oh, how beautiful it will be when we are all together, when this and that person will walk with me… I will exult in that moment!" To bring you an example that can help us better understand, it's like when a girl or a boy think of their beloved: "when we will be together, when we marry…". It's God's dream God thinks of each of us and loves each of us. He dreams about us. He dreams of how he will rejoice with us. That's why the Lord wants to 're-create' us, He wants to renew our hearts so that joy can triumph: have you thought about it? The Lord dreams of me! He thinks of me! I am in the Lord's mind and in his heart! The Lord can change my life! And he has many projects: "we will build houses and plant vineyards, we will share our meals"… these are the dreams of someone who is in love…. Thus we can see that the Lord is in love with his people. And when he says to his people: "I haven't chosen you because you are the strongest, the biggest, the most powerful. I have chosen you because you are the smallest of them all.

You could add: the most miserable. This is whom I have chosen. This is love." God is in love with us. I don't think a theologian exists who can explain this: it is impossible to explain. We can only think about it, we can feel, we can cry with joy. The Lord can change us. "And what must I do?" Believe. I must believe that the Lord can change me, that he has the power to do so. To have faith is to make space for God's love, to make space for his power, for God's power. Not for the power of a powerful person, but for the power of one who loves me, who is in love with me and who wants to rejoice with me. This is faith. This is believing: making space for the Lord so that he can come and change me.[2]

This *A-Z of Living for Christ* contains Pope Francis's guide to making space for God's love in our lives. The Holy Father wants God's dream for each one of us to become a reality and the first step to make this happen is to realise how much he loves each one of us, "For God so loved the world that he gave his only Son, that whoever believes in him should not perish but have eternal life." (*Jn* 3:16)

Deacon Nick Donnelly
Our Lady of Furness parish
Barrow-in-Furness
Feast of St Matthew, Apostle and Evangelist

ADORE · APOSTLE   GUE · BEATIT
· BEAUTY · CELE   · CONVERS
DISCIPLE · DOOR   ST · EVANG
· EXAMINATION   AITH · FAT
FRIENDSHIP · FC   GOSPEL · G
· GRACE · HEAL   POCRISY ·

Adore

To adore. We, in this world of efficiency, have lost the
meaning of adoration, including in prayer. It is true, we
pray, we praise the Lord, we ask, we thank… However,
adoration is being before the One God, the One who
is above price, who does not barter, who does not
exchange… And everything that is outside of him is a
"cardboard imitation", an idol… To adore. In this we must
make an effort to grow in this way of prayer: adoration.
Adore, adore God. This is lacking in the Church at this
moment, because it is not taught. This sense of adoration
that we see in the Bible in the First Commandment -
"Adore the one God. You will have no other God. He is
the Only One you must adore…". This "wasting time"
without asking, without praising, also without giving
thanks, only adoring, with the soul prostrated. I don't
know why I feel like saying this to you but I feel I must
say it to you; it comes from within me.[3]

To adore and to serve: two attitudes that cannot be
separated, but must always go hand in hand. To adore the
Lord and to serve others, keeping nothing for oneself.[4]

Apostle

Being apostles of mercy means touching and soothing the wounds that today afflict the bodies and souls of many of our brothers and sisters. Curing these wounds, we profess Jesus, we make him present and alive; we allow others, who touch his mercy with their own hands, to recognise him as "Lord and God" (*Jn* 20:28), as did the Apostle Thomas. This is the mission that he entrusts to us. So many people ask to be listened to and to be understood. The Gospel of mercy, to be proclaimed and written in our daily lives, seeks people with patient and open hearts, "good Samaritans" who understand compassion and silence before the mystery of each brother and sister. The Gospel of mercy requires generous and joyful servants, people who love freely without expecting anything in return.[5]

Attract

Where is your treasure, what are you longing for? Jesus told us: where your treasure is, there will be your heart - and I ask you: where is your treasure? What is the most important reality for you, the most precious reality, the one that attracts your heart like a magnet? What attracts your heart? May I say that it is God's love? Do you wish to do good to others, to live for the Lord and for your brothers and sisters? May I say this? This is the true treasure. But what is God's love? It is not something vague, some generic feeling. God's love has a name and a face: Jesus Christ, Jesus. Love for God is made manifest in Jesus.[6]

Beatitudes

The Beatitudes are the Christian's identity card. Reread those pages of the Gospel in order to live to the fullest a plan of holiness that goes against the grain of the world's mentality. "How does one become a good Christian?", the answer is simple: do what Jesus says in his discourse on the Beatitudes. A discourse which really goes "against the grain" of what is generally the norm. The Lord knows sin and grace, and he knows the paths that lead to sin and to grace. This is the path, he explained, to live the Christian life in a holy way. The saints did nothing other than live the Beatitudes and that protocol of final judgement, they are few words, simple words, but practical for everyone, because Christianity is a practical religion, to practise, to do, not to simply think about. Today, if you have a little time at home, pick up the Gospel of Matthew, the fifth chapter: the Beatitudes are at the beginning. And then, in Chapter 25, there are other words of Jesus. It will do you good to read this plan of holiness once, twice, three times.[7]

Beauty

The Lord was able to invite others to be attentive to the beauty that there is in the world because he himself was in constant touch with nature, lending it an attention full of fondness and wonder. As he made his way throughout the land, he often stopped to contemplate the beauty sown by his Father, and invited his disciples to perceive a divine message in things: "Lift up your eyes, and see how the fields are already white for harvest" (*Jn* 4:35). "The kingdom of God is like a grain of mustard seed which a man took and sowed in his field; it is the smallest of all seeds, but once it has grown, it is the greatest of plants" (*Mt* 13:31-32).[8]

Those who are dedicated to the defence and the promotion of life may show first and foremost its beauty. Indeed, just as the Church grows not by proselytism but by attraction, human life is defended and promoted most effectively only when its beauty is known and shown.[9]

Bite your tongue

Every time your mouth is about to say something that sows discord and divisiveness and to speak ill of another person the sound advice is to "bite your tongue!" I assure you that if you do this exercise of biting your tongue instead of sowing discord, the first few times your tongue will swell, wounded, because the devil helps to do this because it is his work, it is his job to divide![10]

Celebrate

Celebration is not lazily lounging in an armchair, or the euphoria of foolish escape. No, celebration is first and foremost a loving and grateful look at work well done; we celebrate work. Ultimately, the time for celebration is sacred because God is there in a special way. Sunday Eucharist brings to the celebration every grace of Jesus Christ: his presence, his love, his sacrifice, his forming us into a community, his being with us.[11]

Chaste

In this hedonistic world of ours, in this world where only advertising, pleasure, the good life prevail, I tell you: be chaste! Be chaste! In life, all of us have been through times when this virtue was hard to respect. Yet, it is the proof of true love, one that knows how to give life, one that does not try to use others for one's own pleasure. This love makes holy the life of the other person. "I respect you; therefore, I will not use you." It is not easy. We all know how hard it is to get over facile and hedonistic notions of love.[12]

Confess

Forgiveness of our sins is not something we can give ourselves. I cannot say: "I forgive my sins". Forgiveness is asked for, is asked of another, and in Confession we ask for forgiveness from Jesus. Forgiveness is not the fruit of our own efforts but rather a gift, it is a gift of the Holy Spirit who fills us with the the wellspring of mercy and of grace that flows unceasingly from the open heart of the Crucified and Risen Christ. One might say: "I confess only to God". Yes, you can say to God "forgive me" and say your sins, but our sins are also committed against the brethren, and against the Church. That is why it is necessary to ask pardon of the Church, and of the brethren in the person of the priest.[13]

Conversion

When Jesus calls one to conversion, he does not set himself up as judge of persons, but he calls from a position nearby. How many times have we also felt the need to effect a change which would involve our entire person! How often do we say to ourselves: "I need to change, I can't continue this way… My life on this path will not bear fruit; it will be a useless life and I will not be happy". How often these thoughts come, how often! And Jesus, who is near us, extends his hand and says, "Come, come to me. I'll do the work: I'll change your heart, I'll change your life, I will make you happy". But do we believe this, yes or no? What do you think: do you believe this or not?[14]

Devil

We who want to follow Jesus, and who by our baptism have taken to the Lord's path, must be well aware of this truth: we too are tempted, we too are objects of the demon's attacks, for the spirit of evil does not want us to become holy, it does not us to bear witness to Christ, it does not want us to be disciples of Christ. What does the spirit of evil do to snatch us away from Jesus' path through temptation? The devil's temptations have three main characteristics, and we have to be aware of them in order to not to fall into his trap. First the temptation begins subtly but then it grows and increasingly grows stronger. Then it infects someone else… it spreads to another and seeks to take root in the community. Finally, to calm the soul, it seeks to justify itself. In short: it grows, spreads and justifies itself.[15]

Disciple

The disciple is ready to put his or her whole life on the line, even to accepting martyrdom, in bearing witness to Jesus

Christ, yet the goal is not to make enemies but to see God's word accepted and its capacity for liberation and renewal revealed. Being a disciple means being constantly ready to bring the love of Jesus to others, and this can happen unexpectedly and in any place: on the street, in a city square, during work, on a journey.[16]

To undertake the discipleship of Jesus means to take up your cross - we all have it - to accompany him on his path, an uncomfortable path that is not of success or of passing glory, but that which takes us to the true freedom, freedom from selfishness and from sin. It is to operate a clear rejection of that worldly mentality that places one's "I" and own interests at the centre of existence. That is not what Jesus wants from us. Instead Jesus invites us to lose our life for him and the Gospel, to receive it renewed, realised and authentic.[17]

Door

He is the door: the door by which to enter the sheepfold is Jesus. There is no other. The door of Jesus. The Lord thus clearly says: "you cannot enter eternal life by any entryway that is not the door" - that is not Jesus. He is the door of our life - and not only of eternal life, but also of our daily lives. Any decision I take, I take either in the name of Jesus, passing by way of the door of Jesus, or I take it a little - shall we say in simple language - through the smuggler's hatch? We enter the enclosure through the door, which is Jesus.[18]

ADORE · APOSTLE ... UE · BEATIT
· BEAUTY · CELE ... CONVERS
DISCIPLE · DOOR ... ST · EVANG
EXAMINATION ... AITH · FAT
FRIENDSHIP · FO ... GOSPEL · G
GRACE · HEAL ... POCRISY ·

Encounter

I invite all Christians, everywhere, at this very moment, to a renewed personal encounter with Jesus Christ, or at least an openness to letting him encounter them; I ask all of you to do this unfailingly each day. No one should think that this invitation is not meant for him or her, since no one is excluded from the joy brought by the Lord. The Lord does not disappoint those who take this risk; whenever we take a step towards Jesus, we come to realise that he is already there, waiting for us with open arms.[19]

Eucharist

The Eucharist is Jesus himself who gives himself entirely to us. Nourishing ourselves of him and abiding in him through Eucharistic Communion, if we do so with faith, transforms our life, transforms it into a gift to God and to our brothers and sisters. Nourishing ourselves of that "Bread of Life" means entering into harmony with the heart of Christ, assimilating his choices, his thoughts, his behaviour. It means entering into a dynamism of love and becoming people of peace, people of forgiveness, of reconciliation, of sharing in solidarity. The very things that Jesus did.[20]

Evangelise

Evangelisation, is an art and a discipline, not easy, not something that can be done by rote. Accompany them on their journey of faith, that they might grow in faith along their way. We must put ourselves in the other's shoes - not to get in others' way, but to be on the way with them. We all know people far from the Church: what should we tell them? Look, the last thing you need to do is say something! Begin to do, and he will see what you are doing and ask you about it. And when he asks you, then tell him. To evangelise is to give this testimony: I live the way I do, because I believe in Jesus Christ. I awaken in you a curiosity, so you ask me, "But why are you doing these things?" The answer: "Because I believe in Jesus Christ and preach Jesus Christ and not just with the Word - you must proclaim the Word - but with your life".[21]

Examination of conscience

You can perform a practice as old as the Church, but good: the examination of conscience. Who of us, at night, at the end of the day, remains by himself, by herself, and asks the question: what happened today in my heart? What happened? What things have passed through my heart? If we don't do this, we have truly failed to know how to watch and guard our hearts well. The examination of conscience is a grace, because to guard our heart is to guard the Holy Spirit, who is within us.[22]

Faith

Have faith in God... whoever says to this mountain, "Be taken up and cast into the sea," and does not doubt in his heart, but believes that what he says will come to pass, it will be done for him... Whatever you ask in prayer, believe that you will receive it, and you will. Therefore, what will come to pass is exactly what we ask with faith: it is the lifestyle of faith. One could ask: "Father, what must I do for this?" Ask the Lord, but with faith, that he help you do good things. It's simple, but has one condition, which is exactly what Jesus said: "Whenever you stand praying, forgive, if you have anything against any one". Live the faith so as to help others, to be closer to God, the faith that works miracles.[23]

Father

It's through this Father that we receive our identity as children. And when I say "Father" this goes right to the roots of my identity: my Christian identity is to be his child and this is a grace of the Holy Spirit. Nobody can say "Father" without the grace of the Spirit. "Father" is the word that Jesus used in the most important moments: when he was full of joy, or emotion: "Father, I bless you for revealing these things to little children." Or weeping, in front of the tomb of his friend Lazarus: "Father, I thank you for hearing my prayer," or else at the end, in the final moments of his life, right at the very end. "Father." It's about feeling our Father looking at me, feeling that this word "Father" is not a waste of time. [24]

Forgiveness

If you can't forgive, you are not a Christian. You may be a good man, a good woman but you are not doing what our Lord did. What's more, if you can't forgive, you cannot receive the peace of the Lord. And every day when we pray the 'Our Father': "Forgive us as we have forgiven those". It's a condition.[26]

Friendship

Do you wish to say yes to Jesus' invitation to be his disciples? Do you wish to be his faithful friends? The true friends of Jesus stand out essentially by the genuine love; not some "pie in the sky" love; no, it is a genuine love that shines forth in their way of life. Love is always shown in real actions. Do you want to experience his love? Do you want this love: yes or no? Let us learn from him, for his words are a school of life, a school where we learn to love. This is a task which we must engage in every day: to learn how to love.[25]

Generous

One might ask: "Why so much generosity, Lord?" Jesus gives the answer precisely in the Gospel: so as to be children of your Father who is in heaven. If the Father does so, we too are called to do the same in order to be children. This healing of the heart, in other words, leads us to become children. And what does the Father do? "He makes his sun rise on the bad and on the good; he sends rain on the just and on the unjust", because he is the Father of all. [27]

Gospel

The joy of the Gospel fills the hearts and lives of all who encounter Jesus. Those who accept his offer of salvation are set free from sin, sorrow, inner emptiness and loneliness. With Christ joy is constantly born anew. The joy of the Gospel is for all people: no one can be excluded. That is what the angel proclaimed to the shepherds in Bethlehem: "Be not afraid; for behold, I bring you good news of a great joy which will come to all the people (*Lk* 2:10).[28]

22

Gossip

There are so many enemies of gentleness, aren't there? Starting with gossip. When people prefer to tell tales, to gossip about others, to give others a few blows. These are daily events that happen to everyone, and to me too. They are temptations of the Evil One, who does not want the Spirit to create this gentleness in Christian communities. These conflicts always exist, in the family, in the neighbourhood, even among friends. And this is not new life. If I have something to say, let me say it to the individual, not to the entire neighbourhood; only to the one who can remedy the situation.[29]

Grace

Everything is a free gift from God, everything is grace, everything is a gift out of his love for us. Regarding this love, regarding this mercy, the divine grace poured into our hearts, one single thing is asked in return: unreserved giving. If everything has been given to us, then everything must be passed on. How? By allowing that the Holy Spirit make of us a gift for others. The Spirit is a gift for us and we, by the power of the Spirit, must be a gift for others and allow the Holy Spirit to turn us into instruments of acceptance, instruments of reconciliation, instruments of forgiveness. If our life is allowed to be transformed by the grace of the Lord, for the grace of the Lord does transform us, we will not be able to keep to ourselves the light that comes from his face, but we will let it pass on to enlighten others.[30]

Healing

Jesus is passing by and he halts. Jesus' closeness to us makes us see that when we are far from him there is something important missing from our lives. His presence makes us feel in need of salvation, and this begins the healing of our heart.[31]

Hope

The same God who called Abraham and made him go out of his own land without knowing where he was going, is the same God who goes to the cross, to fulfil the promise He made. It is the same God who, in the fullness of time, ensures that the promise would become a reality for all of us. And what unites that first moment to this last moment is the thread of hope. And that which unites my Christian life to our Christian life, from one moment to another, in order to always go forward - sinners, but going forward - is hope. And what gives us peace in bad moments, in the darkest moments of life, is hope. Hope doesn't disappoint: it's always there: silent, humble, but strong.[33]

Humility

There are many beautiful paintings which may help us to contemplate Jesus on the cross. But the reality of it was very different: he was completely torn and bloodied by our sins. Moreover, this is the way that he has taken in order to defeat the serpent in his field. Therefore, look at Jesus' cross, not at those well-painted artistic crosses, but instead at the reality of what the cross was at that time. Look at his path, recalling that he emptied himself and lowered himself in order to save us. This is also the Christian's path. Indeed, if a Christian wants to make progress on the path of the Christian life, he must lower himself, as Jesus lowered himself: this is the path of humility, which means bringing humiliations upon yourself, as Jesus did.[32]

Hypocrisy

Men and women who can't learn how to acknowledge their own faults become hypocrites. All of them? All of them: starting from the Pope downwards: all of them. If a person isn't able to acknowledge his or her faults that person is not a Christian, is not part of this very beautiful work of reconciliation, peace-making, tenderness, goodness, forgiveness, generosity and mercy that Jesus Christ brought to us.[34]

Idol

Even today, there are so many idols, and even today there are so many idolaters, so many who think they are wise. But even among us, among Christians, eh? But among us - we're speaking within the family - they think they're wise, they know everything… They've become foolish and exchange the glory of the incorruptible God with an image: myself, my ideas, my comforts. We all have within ourselves some hidden idol. We can ask ourselves, in the sight of God: what is my hidden idol? What takes the place of God?[35]

It is true that nowadays, to some extent, everyone, including our young people, feels attracted by the many idols which take the place of God and appear to offer hope: money, success, power, pleasure. Often a growing sense of loneliness and emptiness in the hearts of many people leads them to seek satisfaction in these ephemeral idols.[36]

Imitation

The starting point of salvation is not the confession of the sovereignty of Christ, but rather the imitation of Jesus' works of mercy through which he brought about his kingdom. The one who accomplishes these works shows that he has welcomed Christ's sovereignty, because he has opened his heart to God's charity. In the twilight of life we will be judged on our love for, closeness to and tenderness towards our brothers and sisters. Upon this will depend our entry into, or exclusion from, the kingdom of God: our belonging to the one side or the other. Through his victory, Jesus has opened to us his kingdom. But it is for us to enter into it, beginning with our life now, by being close in concrete ways to our brothers and sisters who ask for bread, clothing, acceptance, solidarity. If we truly love them, we will be willing to share with them what is most precious to us, Jesus himself and his Gospel.[38]

Intercession

How often we must have found ourselves praying for someone. But if a person wants the Lord to grant a grace he must go courageously and do what Abraham did with insistence, Jesus himself tells us we must pray like this. Abraham had been with the Lord for twenty-five years, he had acquired familiarity with him so he dared to embark on this form of prayer. Insistence, courage. It is tiring, true, but this is prayer. This is what receiving a grace from God is.[37]

Jesus

Being Christian is not just obeying orders but means being in Jesus, thinking like him, acting like him, loving like him; it means letting him take possession of our life and change it, transform it and free it from the darkness of evil and sin.[39]

In the Paschal mystery of Jesus we see together death and the cure for death, and this is possible through the great love with which God has loved us, through humble love that lowers itself, through service, taking on the condition of servant. Thus Jesus not only took away evil, but transformed it into good. He did not change things with words, but with deeds; not in appearance, but in substance; not superficially, but radically. He made of the cross a bridge to life. We too can win with him, if we choose willing and humble love, which remains victorious for eternity.[40]

Joy

Joy is truly the virtue of a Christian. A Christian is a man or woman who has joy in their heart. Even more: there can be no Christian without joy. Someone might object, saying: "But Father, I have seen many!" These people are not Christians: they say that they are, but they are not, they are missing something. That is why the identity card of a Christian is his joy, the joy of the Gospel, the joy of having been chosen by Jesus, saved by Jesus, regenerated by Jesus; the joy of the hope that Jesus is waiting for us. In the crosses and sufferings of this life, Christians live that joy, expressing it in another way, with the peace that comes from the assurance that Jesus accompanies us, that he is with us. In fact, Christians see that this joy grows with trust in God. They know well that God remembers them, God loves them, God accompanies them and is waiting for them. This is joy.[41]

Judging

Jesus who seeks to convince us not to judge: a commandment that he repeats many times. In fact, judging others leads us to hypocrisy. And Jesus defines hypocrites as those who act as judges. Because, a person who judges gets it wrong, becomes confused and is defeated. One who judges always gets it wrong. He's wrong because he takes the place of God, who is the only judge: taking that place is taking the wrong place! Believing you have the authority to judge everything: people, life, everything. And with the capacity to judge you also assume you have the capacity to condemn. The worst thing is that, in doing this, they put themselves in God's place, and God is the only judge. And to judge, God takes time, he waits.[42]

DORE • APOSTLE   UE • BEATITU
BEAUTY • CELE   • CONVERSIC
SCIPLE • DOOR   IST • EVANGE
EXAMINATION   AITH • FATH
RIENDSHIP • FO   GOSPEL • GO
GRACE • HEALT   OCRISY •

Kindness

Mercy is the fruit of a covenant; that is why God is said to remember his covenant of mercy (*hesed*). At the same time, it is an utterly free act of kindness and goodness (*eleos*) rising up from the depths of our being and finding outward expression in charity. This all-embracing character means that everyone can appreciate what it means to be merciful, to feel compassion for those who suffer, sympathy for those in need, visceral indignation in the face of patent injustice and a desire to respond with loving respect by attempting to set things right. If we reflect on this natural feeling of mercy, we begin to see how God himself can be understood in terms of this defining attribute by which Jesus wished to reveal him to us. God's name is mercy.[43]

Kingdom of God

Jesus said that the Kingdom of God is always in silence, but also in struggle, explaining further that the Kingdom of God, will grow like wheat, not surrounded by things of beauty but in the midst of weeds. But, the Kingdom is there, it doesn't attract attention, it is silent, quiet.

There is the perseverance of so many Christians carrying the family forward: men, women who care for their children, take care of grandparents, who have only fifty cents in their pocket by month's end, but they pray. And the Kingdom of God is there, hidden in that holiness of daily life, that everyday holiness. Because the Kingdom of God is not far from us, it's close. There is also suffering in the Kingdom of God, take for example, the cross: the everyday cross of life, the cross of work, of the family, the cross of carrying on, and this little everyday cross: rejection. Thus, the Kingdom of God is humble, like a seed: humble; but it becomes big by the power of the Holy Spirit. And we have to let it grow within us, without boasting. May the Spirit come, change our soul and lead us forth in silence, in peace, in quiet, in closeness to God, to others, in adoration of God, without pageantry.[44]

Life

Life is a military endeavour. Christian life is a battle, a beautiful battle, because when God emerges victorious in every step of our life, this gives us joy, a great happiness: the joy that the Lord is the victor within us, with his free gift of salvation. But we're all a bit lazy, aren't we, in this battle and we allow ourselves to get carried away by our passions, by various temptations. That's because we're sinners, all of us! But don't get discouraged. Have courage and strength because the Lord is with us.[45]

Light

What is the Christian's battery that brings light? It is simply prayer. You can do so many things, so many works, even works of mercy, you can do many great things for the Church - a Catholic university, a college, a hospital - and they might even build a monument to you as a benefactor of the Church but if you do not pray then none of this will bring light. How many works become dark due to a lack of light, a lack of prayer. This is precisely the oil, it is the battery which gives life to the light.[46]

Little

A relationship exists between God and us, we who are little. God is great and we are little, and so when God wants to choose people, also his people, he always chooses the little ones. So much so that he says to his people: "I chose you because you are the littlest, those with the least power among all the peoples". The supreme example of this dialogue between God and human littleness is to be found in Our Lady, in she who said: "the Lord has looked upon my lowliness", he has looked upon those who are little, he has chosen the little ones.[47]

Love

"By this everyone will know that you are my disciples, if you have love for one another" (*Jn* 13:35). Love, in other words, is the Christian's identity card, the only valid document identifying us as Christians. It is the only valid document. If this card expires and is not constantly renewed, we stop being witnesses of the Master. The true friends of Jesus stand out essentially by the genuine love; not some pie in the sky love; no, it is a genuine love that shines forth in their way of life. Love is always shown in real actions. Those who are not real and genuine and who speak of love are like characters is a soap opera, some fake love story. Do you want to experience his love? Do you want this love: yes or no? Let us learn from him, for his words are a school of life, a school where we learn to love.[48]

Martyr

This is the beauty of martyrdom. It begins with witness, day after day, and it can end like Jesus, the first martyr, the first witness, the faithful witness: with blood. But there is one condition that is necessary for a true witness and that is there must be no conditions.

One of Jesus' disciples said that he would follow him, but only after having buried his father… and the Lord replied: "No! Follow me without conditions". Your witness must be firm; you must use the same strong language that Jesus used: "Your words must be yes, yes, or no, no". This is the language of testimony.[49]

Mary

If we imitate Mary, we cannot keep our arms folded, only complaining, or perhaps dodging the hard work that others do and which is our responsibility. Mary was always with her people supporting the least. She knew loneliness, poverty and exile, and she learned to create fraternity and to make her home in any place where goodness took root. Let us beseech her to give us a poor spirit which is not proud, a pure heart that sees God in the face of the neediest, great patience that we may not shrink when confronted with life's difficulties.[50]

Mercy

Jesus Christ is the face of the Father's mercy. These words might well sum up the mystery of the Christian faith. Mercy has become living and visible in Jesus of Nazareth, reaching its culmination in him. We need constantly to contemplate the mystery of mercy. It is a wellspring of joy, serenity, and peace. Our salvation depends on it. Mercy: the word reveals the very mystery of the Most Holy Trinity. Mercy: the ultimate and supreme act by which God comes to meet us. Mercy: the fundamental law that dwells in the heart of every person who looks sincerely into the eyes of his brothers and sisters on the path of life. Mercy: the bridge that connects God and man, opening our hearts to the hope of being loved forever despite our sinfulness.[51]

Nothing unites us to God more than an act of mercy - and this is not an exaggeration: nothing unites us to God more than an act of mercy - for it is by mercy that the Lord forgives our sins and gives us the grace to practise acts of mercy in his name. Nothing strengthens our faith more than being cleansed of our sins. Nothing can be clearer than the teaching of Matthew 25 and the Beatitude, "Blessed are the merciful, for they will receive mercy" (*Mt* 5:7), for our understanding of God's will and the mission he has entrusted to us.[52]

Narcissism

The heart becomes hardened by becoming closed inside oneself: making a world within oneself. This happens when man is closed inside himself, in his community or in his parish. It is a closing off which can turn round many things: such as pride, sufficiency, thinking that I'm better than others, or even vanity. There are 'mirror' men and women, who are closed within themselves to watch themselves, constantly; they could be defined as religious narcissists. They have hard hearts because they are closed, they aren't open. And they try to protect themselves with these walls they build around themselves.[53]

It is often an effect of the pathology of power, from a superiority complex, from a narcissism which passionately gazes at its own image and does not see the image of God on the face of others, especially the weakest and those most in need. The antidote to this plague is the grace of realising that we are sinners and able to say heartily: "We are unworthy servants. We have only done what was our duty" (*Lk* 17:10).[54]

Neighbour

The command to love God and neighbour, then, is supremely practical; it entails caring for others even to the point of personal sacrifice. By the end of the parable, we see that the neighbour is not so much the man in need, but rather the one who responded to that need with compassion. Jesus tells all of us to be neighbours in this sense: "Go and do likewise". He himself is the model of the Good Samaritan; by imitating his love and compassion, we show ourselves truly to be his followers.[55]

The novelty is in his placing these two commandments together - love for God and love for neighbour - revealing that they are in fact inseparable and complementary, two sides of the same coin. You cannot love God without loving your neighbour and you cannot love your neighbour without loving God.[56]

New Covenant

It is God who reconciles, creating a new relationship with us, a new covenant. And to do this he sends Jesus; the God who reconciles is the God who forgives. The passage from the Letter to the Hebrews 8:6-13, ends with that beautiful promise: "and I remember their sins no more". He is the God who forgives: our God forgives, reconciles, establishes the new covenant and forgives. But how does God forgive? First of all, God always forgives! He never tires of forgiving. It is we who tire of asking forgiveness. But he never tires of forgiving.[57]

Obedience

What does obeying God mean? Does it mean that we must behave like slaves? No, whoever obeys God is free, he is not a slave! And how can this be? It seems like a contradiction, but it is not. In fact, the word 'obey' comes from Latin, and means to listen, to hear others. Obeying God is listening to God, having an open heart to follow the path that God points out to us. Obedience to God is listening to God and it sets us free. In choosing to obey God and not the world, in no way giving in to compromise, the Christian is not alone. Where can we find help in finding the way to listen to Jesus? In the Holy Spirit. It is the Holy Spirit inside of us who gives us the strength to go forward.[58]

Open

What we need is an openness to expanding our hearts. It is precisely shame and repentance that expands a small, selfish heart, since they give space to God to forgive us. What does it mean to open and expand one's heart? First, it means acknowledging ourselves to be sinners and not looking to what others have done. And from here the basic question becomes: "Who am I to judge this? Who am I to gossip about this? Who am I, who have done the same things, or worse?"[59]

Today, Jesus gives a voice to those without a voice and asks each of us an urgent appeal to open our hearts and make our own the sufferings and anxieties of the poor, the hungry, the marginalised, refugees, those defeated by life, those who are rejected by society and the arrogance of the strongest.[60]

Original sin

Our nature is wounded by original sin. It's something we know from experience. Our humanity is wounded; we know how to distinguish between good and evil, we know what is evil, we try to follow the path of goodness, but we often fall because of our weaknesses and choose evil. This is a consequence of original sin, something that actually happened at the origins of mankind.[61]

The words of Genesis reflect our own daily experience: we are constantly tempted to disobedience, a disobedience expressed in wanting to go about our lives without regard for God's will. This is the enmity which keeps striking at people's lives, setting them in opposition to God's plan. Yet the history of sin can only be understood in the light of God's love and forgiveness. Sin can only be understood in this light. Were sin the only thing that mattered, we would be the most desperate of creatures. But the promised triumph of Christ's love enfolds everything in the Father's mercy. The Immaculate Virgin stands before us as a privileged witness of this promise and its fulfilment.[62]

Peace

To understand what true peace is, we need to return to the words of Jesus: "Peace I leave you, my peace I give to you; not as the world gives do I give to you". What is the peace that Jesus gives? It is a Person; it is the Holy Spirit. On the day of the Resurrection, in the Upper Room, Jesus' greeting to his disciples was: "Peace be with you, receive the Holy Spirit". Therefore, Jesus' peace is a Person, it is a great gift. For when the Holy Spirit is in our heart, no one can take away our peace. No one! It is a lasting peace! In the face of so great a gift, what is our task? We have to guard this peace. It is a great peace, a peace that is not mine: it belongs to another Person who gives it to me as a gift, another Person who is in my heart, who accompanies me throughout my life and whom the Lord has given me. [63]

Persecution

Persecution is one of the characteristics, one of the traits of Church, pervading her entire history. It is cruel the way Saul was cruel at the death of Stephen. Saul went into houses, seized Christians and took them away to be judged.

There is, however, also another kind of persecution that is not often spoken about. The first form of persecution is due to confessing the name of Christ and it is thus a clear, explicit type of persecution. The other kind of persecution is disguised as culture, disguised as modernity, disguised as progress: it is a kind of - I would say somewhat ironically - polite persecution. You can recognise when someone is persecuted not for confessing Christ's name, but for wanting to demonstrate the values of the Son of God. Thus, it is a kind of persecution against God the Creator in the person of his children.[64]

Prayer

Prayer is not a magic wand! It helps to preserve our faith in God, and to trust in him even when we do not comprehend his will. In this, Jesus himself - who prayed so much! - is the example. Our Lord's prayer at Gethsemane, where he prayed for the Father to "deliver him from the bitter cup of the Passion." But his prayer is permeated by faith in the Father, and trusts without restraint in his will: But - says Jesus - not as I will, but as you will. The goal of the prayer is of secondary importance; what matters above all is the relationship with the Father. This is what makes the prayer transform the desire and shape it according to the will of God, whatever it may be, because the person who prays first of all aspires to union with God, who is Merciful Love.[65]

Queen

In Mary, God rejoices and is especially pleased. In one of the prayers dearest to Christians, the Salve Regina [Hail Queen of Heaven] we call Mary "Mother of Mercy". She has experienced divine mercy, and has hosted in her womb the very source of this mercy: Jesus Christ. She, who has always lived intimately united to her Son, knows better than anyone what he wants: that all men be saved, and that God's tenderness and consolation never fail anyone. May Mary, Mother of Mercy, help us to understand how much God loves us.[67]

We implore the Blessed Virgin Mary, under the name "Our Lady of Guadalupe" - the Mother of God, our Queen, our Lady, the young woman, our Little One (as called St Juan Diego called her), and with all the loving names which popular piety has given her - that she may continue to accompany, help and protect our people. May she lead by the hand all pilgrim children in these lands to the encounter with her Son, Jesus Christ, Our Lord, present in the Church, in its holiness, especially in the Eucharist, present in the treasure of his Word and teachings, present in the faithful and holy people of God, in those who suffer and in the humble of heart. So be it. Amen![68]

Question

One only understands the question posed to Peter - "Who am I for you?" - within the context of a long journey, after having travelled a long path. A path of grace and of sin. It is the disciple's path. In fact, following Jesus enables us to know Jesus. To follow Jesus through our virtues and also through our sins. Always following Jesus! In order to know Jesus, what is needed is not a study of notions but rather a life as a disciple. For in journeying with Jesus we learn who he is… we come to know Jesus as disciples. We come to know him in the daily encounter with the Lord, each day. Through our victories and through our weaknesses. It is precisely through these encounters that we draw close to him and come to know him more deeply.[66]

Reconciliation

By our efforts alone, we cannot be reconciled to God. Sin truly is the expression of the rejection of his love, with the consequence of closing in on ourselves, deluding ourselves into thinking that we have found greater freedom and autonomy. Far from God we no longer have a destination, and we are transformed from pilgrims in this world to "wanderers". To use a common expression: when we sin, we turn away from God. That's just what we do; the sinner sees only himself and presumes in this way to be self-sufficient. Thus, sin continues to expand the distance between us and God, and this can become a chasm. However, Jesus comes to find us like a good shepherd who is not content until he has found the lost sheep, as we read in the Gospel (cf. *Lk* 15:4-6). He rebuilds the bridge that connects us to the Father and allows us to rediscover our dignity as children. By the offering of his life he has reconciled us to the Father and given us eternal life (cf. *Jn* 10:15).[69]

Rich

Jesus stood firmly against richness but not about wealth in and of itself: God, in fact, is rich - he presents himself as rich in mercy, rich in so many gifts - but what Jesus condemns is really the attachment to possessions. Indeed, he clearly states how very difficult it would be for a rich man, in other words, a man attached to possessions, to enter the Kingdom of Heaven. The concept is repeated in an even stronger way: "You cannot serve two masters". In this case, Jesus does not place God in opposition to the devil, but God against wealth, because the opposite of serving God is serving wealth, working for wealth, to have more of it, to be secure. What happens in this case? The riches become security and religion a kind of insurance agency: I'm insured with God here and I'm insured with riches here. But Jesus is clear: This is impossible.[70]

Rosary

Mary accompanies us, struggles with us, sustains Christians in their fight against the forces of evil. Prayer with Mary, especially the Rosary - but listen carefully: the Rosary. Do you pray the Rosary every day? But I'm not sure you do [the people shout "Yes!"]... Really? Well, prayer with Mary, especially the Rosary, has this suffering dimension, that is of struggle, a sustaining prayer in the battle against the evil one and his accomplices. The Rosary also sustains us in the battle.[71]

Shame

Shame is a true Christian virtue, and even human, the ability to be ashamed. We must have trust, because when we sin we have an advocate with the Father, Jesus Christ the righteous. And he supports us before the Father and defends us in front of our weaknesses. But you need to stand in front of the Lord with our truth of sinners, with confidence, even with joy, without masquerading. We must never masquerade before God. And shame is a virtue: blessed shame.[72]

We should ask for the grace to be ashamed; shame that comes from the continuous conversation of mercy with him; shame that makes us blush before Jesus Christ; shame that attunes us to the heart of Christ who made himself sin for me; shame that harmonises each heart through tears.[73]

Sinner

"But, Father, you know," one of you might say to me, "you know that this journey is horrible for me, I am such a sinner, I have committed many sins… how can I encounter Jesus?" And you know that the people whom

Jesus most sought out were the greatest sinners; and they reproached him for this, and the people - those who believed themselves righteous - would say: "this is no true prophet, look what lovely company he keeps! He was with sinners..." And he said: "I came for those in need of salvation, in need of healing". Jesus heals our sins. And along the way Jesus comes and forgives us - all of us sinners, we are all sinners - even when we make a mistake, when we commit a sin, when we sin. And this forgiveness that we receive in Confession is an encounter with Jesus. We always encounter Jesus.[74]

Spirit

The Holy Spirit is the one who moves the Church; he's the one who works in the Church, in our hearts; he is the one who makes each Christian a person different from another, but he creates unity among everyone. The Holy Spirit is the one who leads forward, throws open the doors and sends you to bear witness to Jesus. The Holy Spirit is the one who moves us to praise God, who moves us to pray: "Pray, in us". The Holy Spirit is the one who is in us and who teaches us to look to the Father and call him: "Father". This is how he frees us from the state of orphanhood into which the worldly spirit may lead us. For all these reasons, the Holy Spirit is very important: he is the protagonist of the living Church: he is the one who works in the Church.[75]

Tender

God's grace is something else: it's nearness, it's tenderness. If, in your relationship with the Lord, you don't feel that he loves you with tenderness, this means that you are still missing something, you still don't understand what grace is, you still haven't received the grace that is this closeness. You are righteous because God has come close to you, because God caresses you, because God says these beautiful things to you with tenderness: this is our justice, this nearness of God, this tenderness, this love. And our God is so good that he runs the risk of seeming foolish to us. Indeed, if we had the courage to open our heart to this tenderness of God, how much spiritual freedom we would have! How much!⁷⁶

Thanks

Remember the Gospel of Luke? Jesus heals ten who are sick with leprosy, and then only one returns to say thanks to Jesus. The Lord says, "and the other nine, where are they?" This is also true for us: do we know how to say thanks? In your relationship, and then tomorrow in married life, it is important to keep alive the awareness that the other person is a gift of God, and for the gifts of God to say thank you! And in this inner attitude say thanks to each other for everything. It is not a kind word to use just with strangers, to show you are educated. It is necessary to know how to say thank you, in order to get along well together in married life.[77]

Treasure

What is my treasure? It certainly cannot be riches, as the Lord has said: "Do not store up for yourselves treasures on earth, because in the end you will lose them". What is the treasure that we can take with us to the end of life? You can take what you have given, and only that. "Where your treasure is, there will your heart be also". The Lord has made us look for it, to find it, and to grow. But if our treasure is not close to the Lord, if it is not of the Lord, then our heart is restless. We think: what am I? A weary heart that wants to settle with only three or four things, with a nice bank account? Or do I have a restless heart, which increasingly seeks the things of the Lord?[78]

Unconditional love

Do you realise how much you are worth in the eyes of God? Do you know that you are loved and welcomed by him unconditionally, as indeed you are? Once we lose our sense of this, we human beings become an incomprehensible enigma, for it is the knowledge that we are loved unconditionally by God which gives meaning to our lives.[81]

Understand

"I thank thee, Father, Lord of heaven and earth, that thou hast hidden these things from the wise and understanding and revealed them to babes". Only those with the heart of babes are capable of receiving this revelation. Only those with a humble, meek heart, which feels the need to pray, to open up to God, to feel poor have this capacity. In a word, only those who go forth with the first Beatitude: the poor in spirit. Of course so many can learn science, even theology. However, if they don't do this theology on their knees, humbly, that is, like babes, they can't understand a word. Perhaps they may tell us many things, but they won't understand a word. For only this poverty is capable of receiving the revelation that the Father gives through Jesus.[80]

Unity

Unity is not assembled with glue. There is no such thing as a Church built with glue: the Church is made one by the Spirit. Thus, we have to make room for the Spirit to transform us, as the Father is in the Son, one single thing. To accomplish this objective, Jesus himself gives this advice: "Abide in me". This word too is a grace. Jesus prays: "Father, I desire that they also, whom thou hast given me, may be with me where I am", that they may "behold my glory". Re-read the Gospel of John, Chapter 17, verses 20-26, and consider: Jesus prays, he prays for me, he prayed and prays for me still. He prays with his wounds, before the Father. He does this so we may all be one, as he is with the Father, in unity. This should spur us not to judge, not to do things that work against unity and to follow Jesus' advice to abide in him in this life so that we may abide with him in eternity.[79]

Vanity

Vanity is a temptation against which we must battle our whole life, because it always comes back to take the truth away from us. Vanity is like an onion, with layers that must be removed. You take it, and begin to peel it - the onion - and you peel away vanity today, a little bit tomorrow, and your whole life you're peeling away vanity in order to overcome it. And at the end you are pleased: I removed the vanity, I peeled the onion, but the odour remains with you on your hand. Let us ask the Lord for the grace to not be vain, to be true, with the truth of reality and of the Gospel. How many Christians live for appearances? Their life seems like a soap bubble. The soap bubble is beautiful, with all its colours! But it lasts only a second, and then what? Vanity is a liar, a fantasist that deceives itself and deceives the vain. The vain man begins by pretending to be something, and ends by believing in his pretension. Vanity sows wicked anxiety, takes away peace.[82]

Virtue

If, in fact, one can say that he has faith and charity, it is more difficult to speak about hope:

We are able to say this about faith and charity easily, but when we are asked, "Do you have hope? Do you have the joy of hope?" "But, father, I don't understand, can you explain?" Hope, that humble virtue, that virtue which flows under the water of life, but that bears us up so we don't drown in so many difficulties, so we do not lose that desire to find God, to find that wonderful face which we will all see one day: hope. Hope doesn't disappoint: it is silent, humble, and strong.[83]

Voice

We can run away from God as a Christian, as a Catholic and even as a priest, bishop or Pope, we can all flee from God. This is a daily temptation: not to listen to God, not to hear his voice, not to hear his promptings, his invitation in our hearts. And why did Jonah flee from God? And in the parable of the Good Samaritan, why did the priest flee from God? Why did the Levite flee from God? Because their hearts were closed. When your heart is closed you cannot hear the voice of God. Instead, it was a Samaritan on a journey who saw the wounded man and had compassion. His heart was opened, he had a human heart. His humanity enabled him to draw near.[84]

Walk

Holiness means "to walk in the presence of God without reproach". Holiness is a journey; holiness cannot be bought. It can't be sold. It cannot be given away. Holiness is a journey to God's presence that I must make: no one else can do it in my name. I can pray for someone to be holy, but he's the one who has to work towards holiness, not me. Walk in God's presence, in an impeccable way.[85]

Weakness

"In our weakness, we can do nothing without your help". These words express our awareness that we are weak. It is this weakness that we all have, after the wound of original sin: we are weak, we slide into sins, we cannot go forward without the Lord's help. This is why recognising and confessing our weakness is truly indispensable. Indeed, one who thinks he is strong, who thinks he can do it on his own, is at least naïve and, in the end, is a man defeated by so many weaknesses which he carries within himself. Instead, weakness leads us to ask the Lord for help, since, as recited in the collect prayer, "in our weakness, we can do nothing without your help". Thus, we cannot take a step in Christian life without the Lord's help, because we are weak. And a person who is standing must be careful not to fall because she is weak, also weak in faith". Remember, that father who, after the Transfiguration, brings his son for Jesus to heal him. And Jesus says that all is possible for those who have faith. The father responds: "I have faith, but make it grow, Lord, for I am weak!" We all have faith and we all want to move forward in the Christian life. But if we are not conscious of our weakness we will all end up defeated. This is why, this prayer is beautiful: "Lord, I know that in my weakness I can do nothing without your help".[86]

Wounds

Our wounds, those which sin leaves in us, are healed only through the Lord's wounds, through the wounds of God made man who humbled himself, who emptied himself. This is the mystery of the cross. It is not only an ornament that we always put in churches, on the altar; it is not only a symbol that should distinguish us from others. The cross is a mystery: the mystery of the love of God who humbles himself, who empties himself to save us from our sins.[87]

Yearning

We possess within us a yearning for the infinite, and infinite sadness, a nostalgia - the home sickness of Odysseus - which is satisfied only by an equally infinite response. The human heart proves to be the sign of a Mystery, that is, of something or someone who is an infinite response. Outside the Mystery, the needs for happiness, love, and justice never meet a response that fully satisfies the human heart. Life would be an absurd desire if this response did not exist. Only wonder leads to knowledge. If wonder opens me up as a question, the only response is the encounter, and only with the encounter is my thirst quenched. And with nothing else is it quenched more.[88]

Yes

In Mary's "yes" there is the "yes" of all of salvation history and there begins the ultimate "yes" of man and of God: there God re-creates, as at the beginning, with a "yes", God made the earth and man, that beautiful creation: with this "yes" I come to do your will and more wonderfully he re-creates the world, he re-creates us all. It is God's "yes" that sanctifies us, that lets us go forth in Jesus Christ. This is why today is the right day to thank the Lord and to ask ourselves: am I a man or woman of "yes" or a man or woman of "no"? Or am I a man or woman who looks away, so as not to respond?[89]

Zeal

The Lord always wants us to move forward, forward, forward … not to take refuge in a quiet life or in cosy structures, no?… And St Paul, in preaching of the Lord, was a nuisance. But he had deep within him that most Christian of attitudes: Apostolic zeal. He was not a man of compromise. No! The truth: forward! The proclamation of Jesus Christ, forward! And Apostolic zeal is not an enthusiasm for power, for possession. It is something that comes from within, that the Lord wants from us: Christians with Apostolic zeal. And where does this Apostolic zeal come from? It comes from knowing Jesus Christ. Paul found Jesus Christ, he encountered Jesus Christ, but not with an intellectual, scientific knowledge - which is important, because it helps us - but with that first knowledge, that of the heart, of a personal encounter. This is what pushes Paul to keep going, to always proclaim Jesus. He was always in trouble, not in trouble for troubles' sake, but for Jesus, proclaiming Jesus this is the consequence. Apostolic zeal can only be understood in an atmosphere of love. Apostolic zeal implies an element of madness, but of spiritual madness, of healthy madness. Paul had this healthy madness.[90]

Endnotes

[1] Homily at Final World Youth Day Mass, 31st July 2016.

[2] Morning Meditation in the Chapel of the Domus Sancta Marthae, 16th March 2015.

[3] Address to participants in the General Chapter of the Missionary Sons of the Immaculate Heart of Mary, 11th September 2015.

[4] Address to participants in the Plenary Assembly of the International Union of Superiors General, 8th May 2013.

[5] Homily, Feast of Divine Mercy, 3rd April 2016.

[6] Angelus, 11th August 2013.

[7] Morning Meditation in the Chapel of the Domus Sancta Marthae, 9th June 2014.

[8] Encyclical letter, *Laudato Si'*, 97.

[9] Address to the Pontifical Council for Life, 3rd March 2016.

[10] Morning Meditation in the Chapel of the Domus Sancta Marthae, 4th September 2015.

[11] General Audience, 12th August 2015.

[12] Pastoral Visit to Turin. Address to Young People, 21st June 2015.

[13] General Audience, 19th February 2014.

[14] Jubilee Audience, 18th June 2016.

[15] Morning Meditation in the Chapel of the Domus Sancta Marthae, 11th April 2014.

[16] *Evangelii Gaudium*, 24,127.

[17] Angelus, 13th September 2015.

[18] Morning Meditation in the Chapel of the Domus Sancta Marthae, 18th April 2016.

[19] *Evangelii Gaudium*, 3.

[20] Angelus, 6th August 2015.

[21] Morning Meditation in the Chapel of the Domus Sancta Marthae, 9th September 2016.

[22] Morning Meditation in the Chapel of the Domus Sancta Marthae, 10th October 2014.

[23] Morning Meditation in the Chapel of the Domus Sancta Marthae, 29th May 2015.

[24] Morning Meditation in the Chapel of the Domus Sancta Marthae, 16th June 2016.

[25] Homily for the Jubilee Mass for Teens, 24th April 2016.

[26] Morning Meditation in the Chapel of the Domus Sancta Marthae, 10th September 2015.

[27] Morning Meditation in the Chapel of the Domus Sancta Marthae, 14th June 2016.

[28] *Evangelii Gaudium*, 1,23.

[29] Morning Meditation in the Chapel of the Domus Sancta Marthae, 9th April 2013.

[30] Homily for the Feast of the Solemnity of the Immaculate Conception, 8th December 2014.

[31] Homily at penitential service, 4th March 2016.

[32] Morning Meditation in the Chapel of the Domus Sancta Marthae, 14th September 2015.

[33] Morning Meditation in the Chapel of the Domus Sancta Marthae, 18th March 2016.

[34] Morning Meditation in the Chapel of the Domus Sancta Marthae, 11th September 2015.

[35] Morning Meditation in the Chapel of the Domus Sancta Marthae, 15th October 2013.

[36] Homily at the Basilica of the Shrine of Our Lady of the Conception of Aparecida, 24th July 2013.

[37] Morning Meditation in the Chapel of the Domus Sancta Marthae, 1st July 2013.

[38] Homily for Christ the King canonisation Mass, 23rd November 2014.

[39] General Audience, 10th April 2013.

[40] Homily at Mass for the repose of souls of cardinals and bishops who died over the course of the year, 3rd November 2015.

[41] Morning Meditation in the Chapel of the Domus Sancta Marthae, 23rd May 2016.

[42] Morning Meditation in the Chapel of the Domus Sancta Marthae, 23rd June 2014.

[43] Spiritual Retreat given on the occasion of the Jubilee for priests, 2nd June 2016.

[44] Morning Meditation in the Chapel of the Domus Sancta Marthae, 13th November 2014.

[45] Morning Meditation in the Chapel of the Domus Sancta Marthae, 30th October 2014.

[46] Morning Meditation in the Chapel of the Domus Sancta Marthae, 7th June 2016.

[47] Morning Meditation in the Chapel of the Domus Sancta Marthae, 1st January 2014.

[48] Homily for the Jubilee Mass for Teens, 24th April 2016.

[49] Morning Meditation in the Chapel of the Domus Sancta Marthae, 30th June 2014.

[50] Message to the President of the Cuban Episcopal Conference on the occasion of the Day of the Nativity of the Blessed Virgin Mary, 8th September 2014.

[51] *Misericordiae Vultus*. Bull of Indiction of the Extraordinary Jubilee of Mercy, 1st April 2015.

[52] Spiritual retreat on the occasion of the Jubilee for priests, 2nd June 2016.

[53] Morning Meditation in the Chapel of the Domus Sancta Marthae, 9th January 2015.

[54] Presentation of the Christmas greetings to the Roman Curia, 22nd December 2014.

[55] General Audience, 27th April 2016.

[56] Angelus, 26th October 2014.

[57] Morning Meditation in the Chapel of the Domus Sancta Marthae, 23rd January 2015.

[58] Morning Meditation in the Chapel of the Domus Sancta Marthae, 11th April 2013.

[59] Morning Meditation in the Chapel of the Domus Sancta Marthae, 17th March 2014.

[60] Angelus, 28th August 2016.

[61] *The Name of God is Mercy*, p.40.

[62] Homily for the Extraordinary Jubilee of Mercy and Opening of the Holy Door, 8th December 2015.

[63] Morning Meditation in the Chapel of the Domus Sancta Marthae, 20th May 2014.

[64] Morning Meditation in the Chapel of the Domus Sancta Marthae, 12th April 2016.

[65] General Audience, 25th May 2016.

[66] Morning Meditation in the Chapel of the Domus Sancta Marthae, 20th February 2014.

[67] Homily for Feast of Our Lady of Guadalupe, 12th December 2015.

[68] Homily for Feast of Our Lady of Guadalupe, 12th December 2014.

[69] Jubilee Audience, 30th April 2016.

[70] Morning Meditation in the Chapel of the Domus Sancta Marthae, 19th October 2015.

[71] Homily for the Assumption of the Blessed Virgin Mary, 15th August 2013.

[72] Morning Meditation in the Chapel of the Domus Sancta Marthae, 29th April 2013.

[73] Homily on the occasion of the Feast of St Ignatius of Loyola, 31st July 2013.

[74] Homily on the occasion of a pastoral visit to the Roman parish of St Cyril of Alexandria, 1st December 2013.

[75] Morning Meditation in the Chapel of the Domus Sancta Marthae, 9th May 2016.

[76] Morning Meditation in the Chapel of the Domus Sancta Marthae, 11th December 2014.

[77] General Audience, 14th February 2014.

[78] Morning Meditation in the Chapel of the Domus Sancta Marthae, 21st June 2013.

[79] Morning Meditation in the Chapel of the Domus Sancta Marthae, 21st May 2015.

[80] Morning Meditation in the Chapel of the Domus Sancta Marthae, 2nd December 2014.

[81] Message for the Thirtieth World Youth Day 2015.

[82] Morning Meditation in the Chapel of the Domus Sancta Marthae, 25th September 2015.

[83] Morning Meditation in the Chapel of the Domus Sancta Marthae, 17th March 2016.

[84] Morning Meditation in the Chapel of the Domus Sancta Marthae, 7th October 2013.

[85] Morning Meditation in the Chapel of the Domus Sancta Marthae, 24th May 2016.

[86] Morning Meditation in the Chapel of the Domus Sancta Marthae, 18th June 2015.

[87] Morning Meditation in the Chapel of the Domus Sancta Marthae, 8th April 2014.

[88] Jorge Bergoglio, 'For Man' in Elisa Buzzi, *Generative Thought: An Introduction to the Works of Luigi Giussani*.

[89] Morning Meditation in the Chapel of the Domus Sancta Marthae, 4th April 2016.

[90] Morning Meditation in the Chapel of the Domus Sancta Marthae, 16th May 2013.

A-Z of Spiritual Living
By Gerard Bogan

'Spirituality' is a buzzword in our time, yet there is still much confusion about what it means. Arranged alphabetically by spiritual themes, Gerard Bogan opens the spiritual life to a world that is in danger of losing its sense of the divine or the spirit within; a world that has become uncertain about God but seeks God nonetheless – as evidenced by our unconscious daily thoughts and actions. Whether you are a Catholic, or of another faith, or whether you consider yourself to be 'spiritual but not religious', this practical resource is a rich source for reflection.

SP48 ISBN: 978 1 78469 118 9

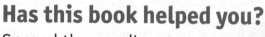